# See for Yourself

*To Kyle and Kirsty*



Published by
**The Bible Reading Fellowship**
Peter's Way, Sandy Lane West
Oxford OX4 5HG
ISBN 1 84101 102 9

First edition 2000
10 9 8 7 6 5 4 3 2 1 0



**Acknowledgments**
Unless otherwise indicated, scripture quotations are taken from the Good News Bible published by The Bible Societies/HarperCollins*Publishers* Ltd UK © American Bible Society, 1966, 1971, 1976, 1992.
Scripture quotations taken from the *Holy Bible, New International Version*, copyright © 1973, 1978, 1984 by International Bible Society. Used by permission of Hodder & Stoughton Ltd. All rights reserved. 'NIV' is a registered trademark of International Bible Society. UK trademark number 1448790.
*The Living Bible* copyright © 1971 by Tyndale House Publishers.

A catalogue record for this book is available from the British Library.

Printed and bound in Great Britain by Caledonian Book Manufacturing International, Glasgow.

Beginning with God

# See for Yourself

*Exploring the Bible with 5-7s*

Rachel Heathfield

# A note to parents and carers

This material is to be used ideally with some help. It is designed to help you to talk to your child about God-things and to learn together.

Every session begins with an idea for looking back at the day and thinking of something or someone in particular. That thing or person is then to be prayed for. Encourage your child to voice their prayer, even if it is just a name or word.

The next bit is to enable you to talk together about a topic which will help you to understand what the Bible verse of the day is about. There are no right or wrong answers here, simply ideas to get you thinking on the right lines. Do not be afraid of difficult questions your child might raise; just be as honest as you can.

There is always a suggestion of something to do, which varies from matching up pictures to organizing a time to get up and see the sunrise. This section is deliberately worded so that the activity doesn't have to happen at that moment—particularly if you do the sessions at bed-time! Please support your child by helping him or her to do the activity, and give a reminder of why that activity was suggested.

*Explore the Bible* is designed to bring together the talking and doing you have just worked through. It might raise more questions, and the answers should be made easier by referring back to the talking bit.

The last part of the session is for the child to complete their own prayer journal on the pages provided. Each session has a linked thought and prayer suggestion. Again, this can be completed straightaway or at another time. Some children might need help; others might like to do it on their own.

I hope you enjoy this material, and may God bless the time you spend with your child exploring the Bible together.

*Rachel Heathfield*

# Perfect dad

## Looking back

In the day just gone, what was the funniest thing that happened?

Thank God for laughter.

## To talk about

What would be a perfect day for you? What would you do? Where would you be?

What would be a perfect meal? Or a perfect holiday?

## Explore the Bible

> **You must be perfect—just as your Father in heaven is perfect!**
>
> *Matthew 5:48*

When we use the word 'perfect' we are often talking about something we like. Someone else might not think that that thing is perfect.

At other times, the word 'perfect' describes the quality of something. It means that that thing is not spoilt in any way. The Bible calls God 'a perfect father'. God is our heavenly dad. He is better than the best dad ever—totally unspoilt.

## To do

Which of these things are perfect and which are spoilt? Draw a line from each picture to the best word to describe it.

Clean torn good chipped new scratched perfect messy

# Prayer jotter

In what things is God perfect?
Write them down here.
In what things can we be perfect?
Write them down here.
Ask God to help you with those things.

# His name is special

## Looking back

Who looks after you at home? Thank God for them and what they do.

Is there anything you can do that would help them? Ask God to show you how you can help them.

## To talk about

Have you ever been called names? Do you know anyone who is called names? Were the names nice or nasty?

Describe what it feels like to be called by a nasty name.

## Explore the Bible

**This, then, is how you should pray:**
**'Our Father in heaven:**
**May your holy name be honoured.'**

*Matthew 6:9*

Some people use God's name badly and some use it as a bad word when they are cross. God doesn't like this and he doesn't deserve it.

God is so special, we need to use his name properly. His name is a sign of what he is like. We need to make sure we always use his name for the right reason—to give him thanks and praise.

## To do

Colour in or design a pattern in this outline of God's name to show how special you think he is.

# Prayer jotter

Think of all the different names you have heard for God and put them down here. If you don't know what they mean, ask someone to help you. Think about them and tell God how great he is, using the names.

# Giver of gifts

## Looking back

Do you know anyone who is ill? Ask God to be with them.

Pray for all the people in hospital and for the doctors and nurses who look after them.

## To talk about

Think about asking for things. When do you ask? What do you ask for? Who do you ask?

Do you always get what you ask for? Why do people give you things? Think about everyday things as well as Christmas and birthdays.

## Explore the Bible

**How much more, then, will the Father in heaven give the Holy Spirit to those who ask him!**

*Luke 11:13*

This verse tells us that God gives us really good things. One of the best things he gives us is his Holy Spirit to be our friend and guide.

People who give us something usually give because they know we need it and they care for us. God is the same—he gives us what we need because he loves us.

## To do

Here are some people asking for things. Match them up with what they want.

# Prayer jotter

God gives us his Holy Spirit—one of the best gifts ever. But he also gives other things.

Think of what you need. What are the things God will give you because he loves you? Are they objects we can touch or are they inside-needs? Ask him for those things.

# He knows you

## Looking back

Think about what you have done and the people you have met in the day just gone.

Thank God for the good bits. Ask him to help you to learn from the bad bits. Say sorry for the things you did wrong.

## To talk about

Who knows the most about you? What do they know? Is there anything they don't know? Why do they know these things?

## To do

Here are some questions about you and your life so far. Now ask the person who you think would know the answers.

- What was my favourite food when I was a baby?
- Have my hair and eyes changed colour since I was a baby?
- What was I like on my first day of school?
- Who was my first friend?
- How many hairs have I got on my head?

## Explore the Bible

> **Not one sparrow falls to the ground without your Father's consent. As for you, even the hairs of your head have all been counted. So do not be afraid; you are worth much more than many sparrows!**
>
> *Matthew 10:29–31*

I bet the person you asked the questions of knew all sorts of things about you, because they love you and care for you.

God knows even more about you. He even knows how many hairs you have! He loves you and thinks you are worth so much that he knows every detail. So don't ever be afraid, God is there with you!

# Prayer jotter

If God knows how much hair you have, what else does he know? All the secrets in your heart; all the fears and wishes you have?

He loves you so much and, because he knows already, it means you can share those things with him.

Draw or write about what it feels like to be known so well.

# God's son

## Looking back

What is your favourite animal? What do you like about it?

Tell God what you think of all the animals he created.

## To talk about

Do you know any children who look just like their parents? Do you look like yours?

Have you ever spotted things other children do or say which are like their parents? Have people said that about you?

## Explore the Bible

**As soon as Jesus was baptized... a voice said from heaven, 'This is my own dear Son, with whom I am pleased.'**

*Matthew 3:16 and 17*

Jesus is God's son. This means that Jesus is like his father. Whatever God loves and does, Jesus does the same.

Jesus was totally a person, but also totally God. As God's son, Jesus is like God.

But he is more than being *like* God, he *is* God.

## To do

Children are often like their parents in the things they do and the things they like.

Match up the children and their parents.

# Prayer jotter

It is hard for us to understand that Jesus can be totally human *and* totally God. But believing in God is about using our inside eyes to see what is not immediately obvious. Ask God to help you believe by opening your inside eyes to see him. Write down what you want to say to him here.

# Father to the fatherless

## Looking back

What were you wearing today? Thank God for your clothes.

Ask God to be with those people who have only one set of clothes.

## To talk about

Not all children live with their parents. This might be because one or both of their parents lives somewhere else, or their parents might have died.

Some people have extra parents because of a second marriage. Talk about your family and about the families your friends live in.

What is your family like? What do you think it would be like to live in a different family?

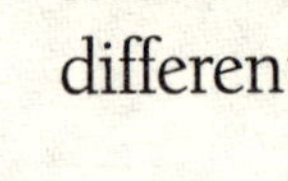

## To do

No two families or households are exactly the same. All families are different because they have different people in them.

Here are some pictures of some families. The blank one is for you to draw in who you live with.

## Explore the Bible

**A father to the fatherless, a defender of widows, is God in his holy dwelling. God sets the lonely in families.**

*Psalm 68:5 and 6 (NIV)*

A human family is the place where we live our human life. But we also have a heavenly father and a heavenly family. God loves us totally, and he loves all our family members. This love never changes—wherever we, or our family members, live.

# Prayer jotter

Sometimes thinking about our family makes us happy, sometimes it makes us sad. How do you feel today? Tell God about it and tell him how it feels to know that he is our dad in heaven. Write or draw how you feel here.

# Divine authority

## Looking back

Think about all of your family—even those who don't live with you. Is there anyone who needs to know God's love for them at the moment? Ask God to be with them.

## To talk about

Do you know what 'authority' is? Ask a grown-up if you don't know.

Who is in authority at school? Who is in authority at home? Think of other people in authority.

## Explore the Bible

**Jesus of Nazareth was a man whose divine authority was clearly proven to you by all the miracles and wonders which God performed through him.**

*Acts 2:22*

Jesus was a person. He was born as a baby, just like you and me. But he also had a special authority—a divine authority. That means that Jesus' authority was given to him by God. God put him in charge of everything. We see what that divine authority means by looking at the special things Jesus did and said which are written about in the Bible.

## To do

Here are some people in authority over something. Match them up with what they are in charge of.

# Prayer jotter

Think and draw something that people do that goes against Jesus' authority. It could be things like fighting and wars, spoiling nature and letting people go hungry. You might think of other things, too.

Pray for those things, asking God to help people do the right thing.

# Jesus died

## Looking back

Sometimes we do things without thinking—things that upset or hurt people. If you have done something like this recently, say sorry to God and ask him to forgive you.

## To talk about

Do you know of someone who has died? Have you ever had a pet that died?

What do we feel when someone we know dies? What do we do when someone dies?

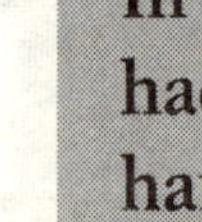

## Explore the Bible

**In accordance with his own plan God had already decided that Jesus would be handed over to you; and you killed him by letting sinful men crucify him.**

*Acts 2:23*

We remember Jesus' death especially at Easter time. But it is not something to think about just at Easter. Jesus' death is very important for two big reasons. First of all, God knew that Jesus would die. Secondly, Jesus didn't stay dead. He came alive again three days later. Wow!

## To do

Here is an Easter picture for you to colour. You can read all about Jesus' resurrection in John's Gospel, chapter 20. You might need to ask a grown-up to help you find it in your Bible and read it with you.

# Prayer jotter

When someone we love dies, we must remember that God is looking after them.

If you know someone who is sad because someone they know has died, ask God to be with them. Maybe you could make them a card.

Draw your ideas for a card here.

# Jesus didn't stay dead

## Looking back

Do you watch television? What is your favourite programme? Thank God for the good things on TV.

## To talk about

Can you think of something impossible? How about jumping to the moon? How about drinking the sea dry?

Think of some more impossible things.

## To do

Beside these pictures, put a tick if they are possible and a cross if they are impossible.

## Explore the Bible

> **But God raised him from death, setting him free from its power, because it was impossible that death should hold him prisoner.**
>
> *Acts 2:24*

The amazing thing about Jesus dying was that he didn't stay dead. God made the impossible happen by making him come alive again. In this verse we see that it was impossible for death to hold Jesus prisoner. His divine authority meant that he just could not stay dead!

This means that if we love Jesus we don't need to be scared about death because we, too, will come alive with Jesus and live again, not on earth, but in heaven.

When someone dies, it is very sad; we miss people when they are not here. But Jesus promises that his friends will never really die, if they believe and trust in him. If you are Jesus' friend, you will have another life in heaven after your life on earth is over.

# Prayer jotter

Talk to God about heaven and
draw or write your thoughts here.

# Exact likeness

## Looking back

Have you played outside recently? What did you do? Was it fun? Tell God about it, thanking him for the things you are able to do.

## To talk about

Can you imagine what it would be like to be so important that everything happens exactly as you say? Can you think of any Very Important People (VIPs) in this country? What happens when they go and visit places?

## Explore the Bible

Christ is the exact likeness of the unseen God. He existed before God made anything at all, and, in fact, Christ himself is the Creator who made everything in heaven and earth, the things we can see and the things we can't.

*Colossians 1:15 and 16 (LB)*

Jesus is so important that everything on earth was made for him. Everything he commanded was done. He is superior to everything. The whole world is under his authority because he is God's Son. The amazing thing is, even though he is such a Very Important Person, we can still know him as our best friend.

## To do

Imagine that you are in charge of the world for the day. What commands would you make?

Make a list, using the pictures here to give you some ideas.

# Prayer jotter

Jesus is the exact likeness of the unseen God. This means that we can know what God is like by looking at Jesus. Even though we can't see Jesus in person today, we can know him by reading about him in the Bible and talking to him in prayer.

What are the best things about knowing who Jesus is? Draw or write them here.

# Amazing!

## Looking back

Who are your best friends? Say their names to God and thank him for them. Tell him why they are your friends.

## To talk about

Think of something amazing. It might be something you heard at school or from a friend or on TV, or something you read about in a book.

The thing you think of might be about how fast something can go or how high something is, or maybe something amazing that your body does. Tell each other amazing things and be amazed!

## Explore the Bible

> **Christ was before all else began and it is his power that holds everything together. He is the head of the body made up of his people—that is, his church—which he began.**
>
> *Colossians 1:17 and 18 (LB)*

Jesus is amazing! He is totally human and totally God at the same time. He has divine authority over everything! He died and came alive again! Everything on earth was made at his command! And now we see in this verse that he existed before all things!

When do you think Jesus became alive?

## To do

Here are some amazing things. Give them marks out of 10 for how amazing you think they are.

- In South America there are spiders whose legs are 25cm long!
- Swifts are birds that never land. They fly all the time, eating and sleeping as they fly.
- Every second of every day and every night, four babies are born somewhere in the world.

# Prayer jotter

This amazing Jesus is also our amazing friend. Draw him and yourself here. Or you could write some words about how amazing you think he is.

# He made peace

## Looking back

Have you ever been to the beach? What is it like?

Thank God for the sea. Ask him to look after all those people on boats who might be in danger.

## To talk about

Have you had any good news in your family recently? What about a new baby? Or someone getting some good exam results?

What is it like getting good news? Do you remember getting any bad news? What was it? Do you get bad news at school? What is that?

## Explore the Bible

**God made peace through his Son's blood on the cross and so brought back to himself all things, both on earth and in heaven.**

*Colossians 1:20*

There is lots of good news in God's big story. God made the world to be brilliant and perfect. He made people to love him, to walk, talk and live in his ways. However, people chose to do their own thing, and their disobedience to God became the bad news in God's good world.

Through Jesus' death, everything can be made good again and we can be friends with God.

## To do

Which of the things in these pictures are good news and which are bad news? Are there any that could be good news for some people and bad news for others?

# Prayer jotter

God 'made friends' with us again through Jesus. Maybe you know what it feels like to break friends.

Ask God to help you with your human friends. Draw a picture of you and your friends here.

Thank God that you and he can now be friends because of Jesus.

# Always there

## Looking back

What was the weather like in the day just gone?

Thank God for the good things the weather does.

## To talk about

What is the oldest thing or place you have ever seen or been to? How do you know that it is old? How old are the mountains? Or the hills?

Can you imagine a time when the hills and mountains weren't there? They are older than anything built or made.

## Explore the Bible

**O Lord, you have always been our home. Before you created the hills or brought the world into being, you were eternally God, and will be God for ever.**

*Psalms 90:1–2*

It is hard for us to understand how time works. Some very clever people are still trying to work out how things get old. Do you know that the oldest something can be is if it has always been there? This verse tells us that even before the world was made, before this earth began, God was there. He has always been there.

## To do

Put these things in age order:
young, old, older, oldest.

# Prayer jotter

Some things about God are so clever that we will never understand them. This is because God is cleverer than the cleverest person in the world!

Draw or write about the things you don't understand. Praise God that he is so clever!

# The helper

## Looking back

Who is in your family? Thank God for them.

Ask him to be with those who especially need him at the moment.

## To talk about

If you want to know something, who do you ask? Who helps you to understand things?

What do you most like learning about?

## To do

Look at these people. What would they help you to know and understand? Join the person to the thing they could help you with.

## Explore the Bible

**I will ask the Father, and he will give you another Helper, who will stay with you for ever. He is the Spirit who reveals the truth about God.**

*John 14:16 and 17*

In this verse Jesus tells us that he will send us a helper who will come and help us to know and understand God. That helper is the Holy Spirit. The Holy Spirit's job is to help us to understand. He will always be with us to show us the truth about God.

Think about how it feels when your mind suddenly works something out. Are there things at school that your mind is still trying to work out?

The Holy Spirit often waits until we are ready to understand. This could be after a short time or a long time.

# Prayer jotter

The Holy Spirit comes to help us work out what God is like. What do you want to understand?

Write or draw it and ask God to send his Holy Spirit to help you to understand.

# Like the wind

## Looking back

Think about the wind and what it does. What do you like to do on a windy day?

Thank God for the wind and what we can do in it.

## To talk about

Do you like the wind? What does it feel like? Where do you notice it? What does the wind do to things?

Can you see the wind? Can you touch the wind?

## To do

Here are some things that need the wind. What happens to them when it's windy?

## Explore the Bible

> **The wind blows wherever it wishes; you hear the sound it makes, but you do not know where it comes from or where it is going. It is like that with everyone born of the Spirit.**
>
> *John 3:8*

We can't see the wind, only what it does to things. In the same way, Jesus says we can't see God's Holy Spirit, only what it does to people.

God's Holy Spirit helps people to understand God, which helps them to live in a way that pleases him. If we live a life that pleases God, it shows others that the Holy Spirit is with us.

# Prayer jotter

Is it easy to please God? Can you think of something you need the Holy Spirit to help you with? It might be being kind to someone, or not getting angry.

Draw or write about it here. Ask God to be with you through his Holy Spirit.

Week 3 Session 4

# Tongues of fire

## Looking back

Have you seen anyone crying recently? Is the thing that made them cry sorted out and cleared up now?

Pray for people who are sad.

## To talk about

What does fire do? When is it safe and when is it dangerous? Where in the house do we find flames? Are they safe flames? What are the flames for?

Where in the house do you find heat? What does that heat do?

## Explore the Bible

**Then they saw what looked like tongues of fire which spread out and touched each person there. They were all filled with the Holy Spirit.**

*Acts 2:3 and 4*

God wants us to understand who the Holy Spirit is. The Bible explains it by saying he is like the wind. Here we see that the Holy Spirit is like fire. The Holy Spirit's flames weren't dangerous because they didn't burn anything up. But the flames did change people. Cold food becomes hot so it can be eaten. Wet clothes become dry so they can be worn. The Holy Spirit changes people so they can be like Jesus.

## To do

Here are some things that need heat. What type of heat do they need? How do we use them when they have been heated?

# Prayer jotter

When the Holy Spirit came, looking like tongues of fire, it must have been amazing. See if you can draw tongues of fire in the space here.

# Christian fruit

## Looking back

What is your favourite time of year? Why?
Is it now? Thank God for that special time.

## To talk about

What tree produces apples? What kind of bush has raspberries? How can you know that a tree is an oak tree? Would a pear tree ever give you bananas? Why?

## Explore the Bible

**The Spirit produces love, joy, peace, patience, kindness, goodness, faithfulness, humility and self-control.**

*Galatians 5:22 and 23*

Just as an apple tree has the right fruit, the Bible says that a Christian is like a tree that has Christian fruit. When the Holy Spirit lives in us, he makes our lives show that we love God.

We look at an apple tree and see apples. We look at someone who loves God and see the things that his Holy Spirit produces.

## To do

Join up the fruit to its tree or plant.

Fill in the names of the Christian fruit in the tree on the prayer jotter. God will make these things grow in us. Have you seen them in other people? Have you seen them in yourself?

# Prayer jotter

Week 3
Session 6

# Promised by God

## Looking back

Look out of a window near you. What can you see?

Praise and thank God for it.

## To talk about

What is a promise? What promises do you make? Do you keep them? Who has made promises to you? Have they kept them?

## Explore the Bible

> **God says: I will pour out my Spirit on everyone.**
>
> *Acts 2:17*

God promises that he will give everyone his Holy Spirit. This means that everyone will receive the Holy Spirit, who helps us to understand God and live a life that pleases him. God keeps his promises. Isn't that a good thing?

## To do

Which of these promises have you made? Have you made promises that are nearly the same?

# Prayer jotter

God never lets us down. He always wants the best for us.

Write a prayer here to thank him for his promises.

# Communication

## Looking back

Do you need to say sorry to God for anything in the day just gone?

God promises that when we say sorry, he forgives us and takes those wrong things away.

## To talk about

Try to think of the many different ways we communicate with people.

Is there anywhere we cannot talk to other people?

## To do

Here are some people communicating. Can you link them to the people they are communicating with?

## Explore the Bible

> **Your word, O Lord, will last for ever; it is eternal in heaven.**
>
> *Psalm 119:89*

God talks to us. But he doesn't use the phone or a computer. One way he talks to us is through the Bible. That is why the Bible calls itself 'God's word'. This verse tells us that God's word lasts for ever. That means it can never be cut off or deleted or lost.

# Prayer jotter

Even when we can't read very well, God still speaks to us. When we hear the Bible read, or see a Bible story on television or on video, God is speaking to us. God talks to us because he loves us.

Thank God for speaking to us through the Bible. Draw something or write a prayer to God in reply.

# Lamps and lights

## Looking back

When did you last go to church? What was the best bit?

Thank God for his church, for the people there and for all the things that happen in church that help us to know God better.

## To talk about

What might it feel like to be lost? Have you ever been out when someone needed to look at a map to find the way? Think about that time.

How easy is it to see where you're going when it's dark? Have you ever used a torch in the dark? Think about that time.

## To do

This beam of light is only lighting up part of something. Can you work out what the thing is?

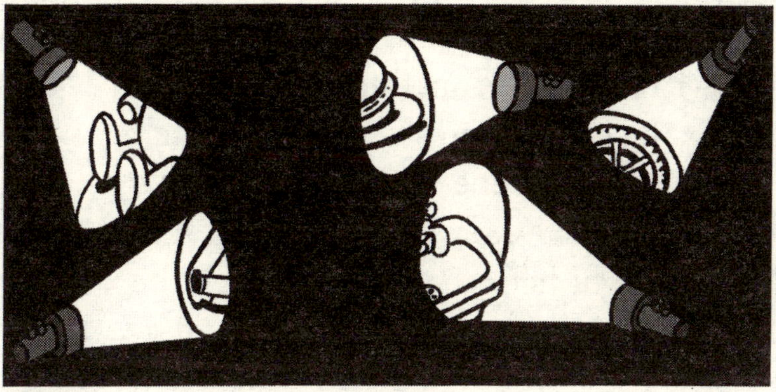

## Explore the Bible

> **Your word is a lamp to guide me and a light for my path.**
>
> *Psalm 119:105*

Sometimes life is complicated and confusing. A bit like a path in the dark—it is hard to know where to go. God's word is like a lamp for the complicated bits of life. It guides us to do the right thing. It helps us to make good decisions.

# Prayer jotter

What feels confusing at the moment? Is anything complicated? If so, God cares and wants to help. Ask someone who knows about the Bible to show you something that might help. That person might be one of your parents, your church leader, your children's group leader at church or your teacher at school. Write or draw here the things you are wondering about.

# Tasty words

## Looking back

What did you do in the day just gone?

Thank God for the funniest bit. Thank him for the most exciting bit.

## To talk about

What is your favourite food? What does it taste like? How do you feel after a really good meal?

What does food make our bodies able to do?

## To do

Set up a taste test for someone at home. You might need to do this another time. Have a few bits of food ready and blindfold your volunteer. Bring them a little bit of the food. Can they guess what it is just by the taste? Try using a little breakfast cereal, some salt, some sugar and some crisps. (Can they guess the flavour?) What else can you find to try?

## Explore the Bible

> **How sweet is the taste of your instructions—sweeter even than honey!**
>
> *Psalm 119:103*

How can words be tasty? This verse is like a picture. Listening to what God tells us to do is like eating a good meal—we are then fit and ready to get on and do it! God's instructions help us in life just like food does. God's word 'feeds' us and helps us grow strong in living a life that is pleasing to him.

# Prayer jotter

Remember that God's word is him speaking to us. What might God tell us that is sweet tasting?

Write or draw it here.

Week 4 Session 4

# Truth and lies

## Looking back

Did you get enough to eat in the day just gone? Thank God for food.

Ask him to be with those who are hungry at the moment.

## To talk about

What is the truth? What is the opposite of true?

What do you learn at school? Is it truth or lies? Would a teacher ever teach you lies?

## To do

Here are some sentences. Work out which are true and which are false. Put a tick by the truth and a cross by the lie.

- God loves us very much
- God's word tells us how to be naughty
- God talks to us through the Bible
- God thinks lying is OK

## Explore the Bible

> **All Scripture is inspired by God and is useful for teaching the truth.**
>
> *2 Timothy 3:16*

'Scripture' is another word for the Bible. Have you heard that word before? This verse tells us that the Bible is good for teaching. The Bible doesn't teach lies, it teaches the truth. That truth tells us the best ways to live and how to please God.

# Prayer jotter

Draw the person who teaches you about God here. Say 'thank you' to God for that person.

# Instruction manual

## Looking back

What are you looking forward to at the moment? What can't you wait for?

Tell God about it and thank him for it.

## To talk about

Do you ever do things wrong? Who tells you that they are wrong? What sort of things do you do wrong?

Sometimes we are trying to do something new and it doesn't work. Where do we go for help?

## To do

How do we find out we've done something wrong? Here are some examples. Can you think of some more?

## Explore the Bible

**All scripture is inspired by God and is useful for rebuking error and correcting faults.**

*2 Timothy 3:16*

Life is sometimes confusing and complicated. The Bible is a bit like an instruction book. God has given it to us so that we can find where we went wrong. That is what this verse reminds us. The Bible also helps us to do the right thing in the first place.

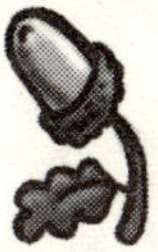

# Prayer jotter

What or who else helps us to live in the way God wants? God loves us very much and wants us to be friends with him. That is why he gives us so much help!

Thank him for the Bible and draw it here.

# Helpful life

## Looking back

Think of different reasons why God is amazing. Now tell him! This is what 'praising God' means.

## To talk about

Think of the times you have helped someone. What did you do? How do you know what was helpful? How did it feel to be helpful?

## To do

Look at these pictures. What would be the helpful thing to do?

## Explore the Bible

**All scripture is inspired by God and is useful for giving instruction for right living, so that the person who serves God may be fully qualified and equipped to do every kind of good deed.**

*2 Timothy 3:16 and 17*

The Bible helps us to think about what is helpful and good. This verse calls this 'right living'. When God's Holy Spirit lives with us, we want to be helpful and kind. Can you remember the fruits of the Spirit on page 55?

The Bible also shows us how to help others by being the person God wants us to be.

Think about the day just gone. Is there anything you could have done to be helpful and good, but you didn't do it? Is this what God wants?

# Prayer jotter

Write or draw a prayer to ask God to help you to do good whenever you see the chance.

# God's signature

## Looking back

Have you learnt anything new today? Was it about the world or about what you can do?

Thank God for it.

## To talk about

Have you ever been to an art gallery? Where? Think of a beautiful painting you might have seen. Maybe it was in a book or hanging on a wall. What was it like?

When we look at a painting, how do we know who painted it?

## Explore the Bible

**Ever since God created the world, his invisible qualities, both his eternal power and his divine nature, have been clearly seen; they are perceived in the things that God has made.**

*Romans 1:20*

This verse tells us that even though we can't see God physically here, we can see him all around us. We can see God in creation because, like the inventors and the painters, we can see where God has left his mark. When we look at a beautiful view, what does it tell us about God? It tells us that he is beautiful and colourful. He loves variety and he made things for us to enjoy!

## To do

When an inventor invents something new, they often leave something in the invention that lets people know it is their invention. Match the inventor with their creation.

# Prayer jotter

Think of your favourite bit of creation. What does it tell you about God? Draw it or write about it here.

# Sky is amazing

## Looking back

Think about yourself. Look at your face in a mirror. There is only one of you in the whole world! Aren't you amazing?

Praise God for making you YOU!

## To talk about

What is the night sky like? How many stars are there in the sky? Where do the stars go during the day?

What colour is night? How different is the sky during the day from the way it is at night-time?

## Explore the Bible

> **How clearly the sky reveals God's glory!**
> **How plainly it shows what he has done!**
>
> *Psalm 19:1*

When you think about the sky, what do you think? The sky is amazing! It's huge! It's got so many colours! It always looks different, day and night! It is full of stars that stay there all the time.

God made the sky, and when we look at it, we see his glory—how amazing, powerful and creative he is. He made the stars and gave them all names! *Wow!*

## To do

Here are some patterns that the stars make. Next time it is dark and cloudless, have a look in the sky to see if you can spot the shapes—they are always there!

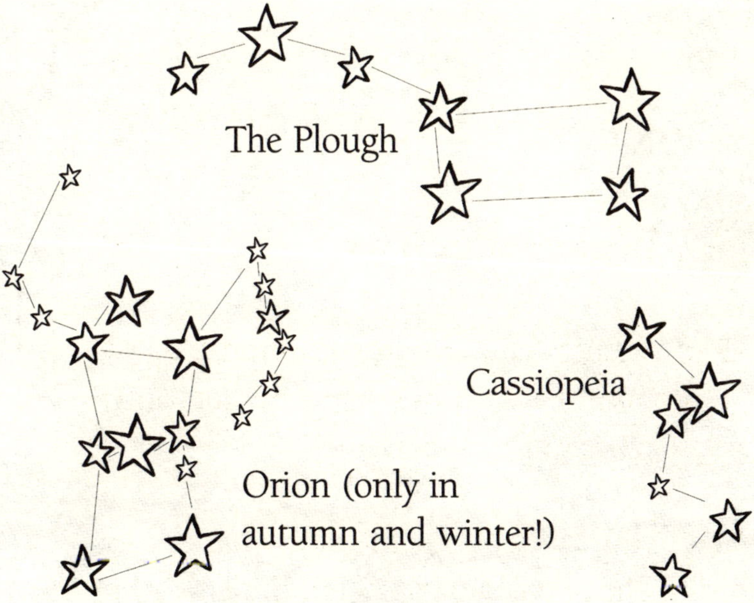

# Prayer jotter

What words can you use to describe the sky? How would you draw the sky? What words would you use to describe God? How would you draw him?

Use this space to write or draw about God and the sky.

# The 'disobedient' earth

## Looking back

Do you like being outdoors? What is good about it?

Thank God for the good things you enjoy out and about.

## To talk about

What happens when a volcano erupts, or a huge wind blows or when there is an earthquake or flood?

Do you think God is happy when these things happen? Do you think he should stop them from happening?

## Explore the Bible

**Yet there was the hope that creation would one day be set free from its slavery to decay and would share in the glorious freedom of the children of God.**

*Romans 8:20 and 21*

Our Bible verse today helps us to understand a little bit about natural disasters. When God made the world, he made it to be perfect. It is sad that just as people started to disobey God—what the Bible calls sin—so the earth also sometimes disobeys God. The earth 'sins' just like people do. However, one day, God will set the earth free from its 'sin', just as he sets people free from their sin.

## To do

Here is a picture of the world; one half is perfect, as God created it, the other half is going wrong, because of sin.

Look at what you can see.

# Prayer jotter

There are people all over the world who have had their lives messed up by a natural disaster. They might have lost their families or their homes.

Pray for them and the people who help them. Pray that God will be with them.

Week 5
Session 4

# Who's in charge?

## Looking back

What do you want to be when you grow up? Ask God to help it to happen.

## To do

Who is in charge here? Join up the groups and the person in charge.

## To talk about

Do you know anyone who is second-in-command? What about the deputy head at school? Who is in charge of this country? Is there someone second-in-charge?

What does it mean to be second-in-command? Is it an important job?

## Explore the Bible

> **You made people inferior only to yourself; you crowned them with glory and honour. You appointed them rulers over everything you made; you placed them over all creation.**
>
> *Psalm 8:5 and 6*

Do you remember talking about Jesus being in charge of the world? This verse tells us that God has made us to be in charge of the animals and plant life. That means that we are second-in-command to Jesus. That is amazing. He thinks so much of us that he put us in charge of all the animals and everything God created. *Wow!*

# Prayer jotter

Draw some of the things you have heard of which show that people are spoiling the creation we are in charge of. Write a prayer about it.

# Treasured possession

## Looking back

Think about farmers. What do they do? Thank God for their hard work that makes our food. Pray that they will be kept safe on the farms.

## To talk about

Have you got anything that you really treasure? What is it? It might be something valuable or delicate, or something you love or have had for a long time. Where do you keep it?

Do you know anyone else with something they really treasure? What do they do with it? How do they look after it?

## Explore the Bible

**Look at the birds: they do not sow seeds, gather a harvest and put it in barns; yet your Father in heaven takes care of them! Aren't you worth much more than birds?**

*Matthew 6:26*

God really treasures his creation. Everything he has made he looks after and cares for. He makes sure everything is safe. In this verse we see that he makes sure everything gets enough to eat.

Remember that God made us in charge of the animals and birds. Because this is so, and God looks after the birds so well, the Bible tells us that he will look after us just as well, if not better. We must never worry about things when we have a heavenly Father taking care of us!

## To do

Here are some people showing how much they treasure things. What are they doing?

# Prayer jotter

Because God asks us to care for his creation, we should try to help people throughout the world who are hungry and poor.

Try to think of ways you can help other people. Draw or write about them here.

# Totally unique

## Looking back

Sometimes our words are mean. Sometimes our words are untrue. How were your words today?

Say sorry to God for the times your words have hurt others and God.

## To talk about

Think about how unique you are.What is your favourite colour? Favourite food? Place? Smell? Sound?

How many other people like that exact combination of things? Look at your face in a mirror. How many freckles or different coloured bits can you see?

Look at your hands. How many lines can you see? There is no one else in the whole world with lines like that on their hands!

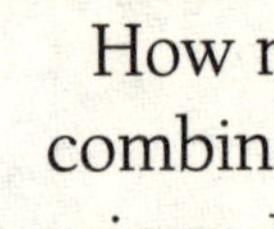

## To do

Take a record of your fingerprints. You will need a felt-tip pen. Colour in just the top part of one finger. Work fairly fast so that you can get a print before the ink dries. Carefully press the finger in the correct box below. Go on and do the next finger. Keep going until you have five prints. Now wash your hands!

| | | | | |
|---|---|---|---|---|
| Thumb | 1st | 2nd | 3rd | 4th |

## Explore the Bible

> **You created every part of me; you put me together in my mother's womb.**
>
> *Psalm 139:13*

Do you remember how we can see God in his creation? One of the clearest and most amazing ways to see God is to look at yourself. No, we are not God! But we are made in his image! We are fantastic! We can do amazing things. We are totally unique. And God knew all about us even before we were born. He knew what we would like and dislike, what we would be good at and not so good at. He put us together just as he wanted us to be.

# Prayer jotter

Sometimes we get sad looking at ourselves because we think we're not as clever or good-looking as someone else. We mustn't think that. God made us to be just right!

Thank God for helping you to see for yourself how great he is and how special you are. Draw a picture of yourself here.